Written by: Illustrated by: Designed by:

Ethan Arabov   Ugur Kose   Mia Hay

Also by Ethan Arabov:
Available on Amazon Now!

Truthful Tammy

Written By: Ethan Arabov

Illustrated By: Ugur Kose

We will always love you

Written by:

Ethan Arabov

Illustrated by:

Ugur Kose

Designed by:

Mia Hay

ISBN: 9798403911313

Mommy and Dad
love me very much
I know it 'cause I feel it

When I feel
their touch

No matter what happens
they're always there
By spending time with me
I know that they care

All of the extra things
like playing with toys
fill my heart up
and add to the joys

I love when they sit
and read me a book
The happiness they have
when I give them the look

They think it's the story
that's making me happy
or when they sing to me
as I'm taking a nappy

I can't describe in words
when they are both around
Whether they are serious
    Or acting like clowns

It can be when they buy me ice cream
and I give it a hundred licks

Or when they clean my boogies
when I'm feeling a little sick

When we all cuddle
and watch a cartoon

or if its my birthday
and they bring me balloons

But Mommy and Dad
started doing things apart
Even though they loved me
it was breaking my heart

It felt a bit weird
to witness it all

So I sat in my
room

and played with my
ball

When Dad had to leave
and took all of his stuff
I had to hold it all in
and pretend to be tough

I won't do it I thought
I won't shed a tear
I won't give in
even if it's loneliness I fear

I'll see you in a bit
as Dad gave me a hug
and sat me down
on our playtime rug

But Mommy
threw a party
for me
my friends and
hers with soda
and tea

The crowd was awesome
but still missing one
I was looking for Dad
Amongst all the
fun

But there in the corner
a familiar face
Mommy its Dad
To him I had
raced!

I can't believe
you're really here
As Dad took his hand
to wipe away my tear

Know that we love you
and all that you are
it'll get better
and won't stay like a scar

Look to the sun
and remember the days
when all we would do
was sit out and play

I will always be around
just give me a call
We'll go to the park
and toss around the ball

Even if at times
we are not together
know that Mommy and I
will love you forever

About The Author:
Ethan Arabov

While so many people dream of a creative career, one man is breaking the mold of artistic pursuits.

Meet Ethan Arabov, musician, marketer, jewelry designer, and children's author most recently.

Born in Queen's, New York, the child of hard-working Russian immigrant parents, Ethan was a quiet child who kept to himself. Endlessly curious and reflective, Ethan never felt he belonged, but he excelled in school and won multiple Golden Presidential Awards for Educational Excellence.

With a background in finance and marketing, Ethan's career has spanned the creative spectrum from celebrated singer/songwriter/producer to graphic artist, jewelry designer, and now children's author.

Art allows me to tell stories. Being artistic and creative gives me a platform to express myself. My writing comes from the heart. I want to put something positive out into the world. Ethan Arabov

When he sang a cover to the Celine Dion/Peabo Bryson song Beauty & the Beast, Ethan was just six.

It wasn't until the age of 15 that Ethan got serious about music. Known for his relatable lyrics, Ethan released his debut album in 2001, with several songs landing #1 on local radio and later won accolades for his hit single Falling in Love. Ethan was never going to be a one-trick pony.

His latest foray into writing makes this clear. Ethan embraces an eclectic mix of heartfelt melodies in music — most of his books have a similar positive vibe.

I love writing. I have been writing since I was a teenager—songs, poems, and now, books. I have a lot of nieces and nephews. I can relate to kids — and sometimes they just need a little encouragement that life will be ok.

Made in the USA
Monee, IL
30 November 2022

19074282R00019